T0151174

WORDS TO SHAKE IT OFF

Published in 2023 by OH!
An Imprint of Welbeck Non-Fiction Limited,
part of Welbeck Publishing Group.
Offices in: London – 20 Mortimer Street, London W1T 3JW
and Sydney – 205 Commonwealth Street, Surry Hills 2010
www.welbeckpublishing.com

Compilation text © Welbeck Non-Fiction Limited 2022
Design © Welbeck Non-Fiction Limited 2022

Disclaimer:

ISBN 978-1-80069-169-8

Compiled and written by: Lisa Dyer
Editorial: Victoria Godden and Laura Garcia Rodriguez
Project manager: Russell Porter
Design: Tony Seddon
Production: Jess Brisley

A CIP catalogue record for this book is available from the British Library

Printed in Italy

THE LITTLE GUIDE TO

TAYLOR SWIFT

WORDS TO SHAKE IT OFF

CONTENTS

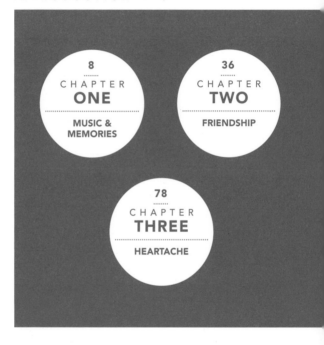

INTRODUCTION

From her girl squad to the Swifties fanbase to the world at large, Taylor's the BFF of the pop music world. As the go-to shoulder to cry on and chronicler of heartbreak, she relates her personal life and experiences in her music, at her live performances, and on her social media feeds. One of the most followed celebrities, she is a defender of the underdog, open about her feminist and pro-choice views, and frequently speaks up against sexism and LGBTQ discrimination. All that, and she also delivers music that could be the soundtrack to our lives—there's something for every situation, mood, and emotion.

A naturally talented singer-songwriter, Taylor went from an idyllic childhood in rural Pennsylvania, performing "The Star-Spangled Banner" before a Philadelphia 76ers basketball game at age 11, to Nashville, signing with Sony/ATV as a songwriter at the age of 14 and getting her first hit, "Tim McGraw", at 16. Originally inspired by country music legends Shania Twain, Faith Hill, and the Dixie Chicks, she soon dominated the music world with her personalized brand of mainstream pop mixed with country roots; her confessional lyrics documenting growing-up themes such as romance and popularity struck a chord with other young women like her.

In this collection of Taylor's relatable, inspiring, and optimistic quotes and lyrics, you will find the best advice on falling in love and getting over it, friendships and feuds, her feelings about songwriting and success, and pearls of wisdom to carry with you through life. Sparkling with positivity and feel-good vibes, Taylor is always there to support you and lift you up when you're down—she's your own personal cheerleader.

CHAPTER
ONE

MUSIC &
MEMORIES

Taylor's early life, family, memories,
and the inspirations behind her music,
in her own words.

I had the most magical childhood, running free and going anywhere I wanted to in my head.

Rolling Stone, March 5, 2009

66

I think I first realized I wanted to be in country music and be an artist when I was 10. And I started dragging my parents to festivals, and fairs, and karaoke contests, and I did that for about a year before I came to Nashville for the first time.

99

Yahoo! Music, October 2006

Born on December 13, 1989,
Taylor Alison Swift grew up
on a Christmas tree farm in
Wyomissing, Pennsylvania before
moving to Hendersonville,
Tennessee, at the age of 14
to break into the country
music scene.

She was named after the singer-
songwriter James Taylor and has
a younger brother, Austin.

My mom and I have always been really close. She's always been the friend that was always there. There were times when, in middle school and junior high, I didn't have a lot of friends. But my mom was always my friend. Always.

99

Great American Country network, 2008

I love writing songs because I love preserving memories, like putting a picture frame around a feeling you once had.

Elle, February 28, 2019

Songs for me are like a message in a bottle. You send them out to the world, and maybe the person who you feel that way about will hear about it someday.

Daily Beast, July 14, 2017

My experience with songwriting
is usually so confessional, it's so
drawn from my own life and my
own stories.

Entertainment Weekly, December 23, 2013

People haven't always been there for me, but music always has.

Twitter, October 8, 2013

I've always felt music is the only way to give an instantaneous moment the feel of slow motion. To romanticize it and glorify it and give it a soundtrack and a rhythm.

The Guardian, October 18, 2012

It doesn't bother me when people try to deconstruct my songs, because at least they're looking at the lyrics and paying attention to the way the story is told.

The Guardian, October 18, 2012

> My glitter nail polish says 'party' but my sweatpants / bun on top of head ensemble say 'room service and journaling my feelings.'

Twitter, October 5, 2012

Sitting on a bedroom floor crying … those are things that make you feel really alone, and if someone's singing a song about that feeling, you feel bonded to that person. That's the only way I can find an explanation for why 55,000 people would want to come see me sing.

Mirror, August 5, 2013

"Lucky You" was the first song Swift ever wrote, at 12 years old.

Local musician and computer repairman Ronnie Cremer taught her to play her first three chords (C, D, and G) on the guitar and that evening she wrote the song.

Music is art, and art is important and rare. Important, rare things are valuable. Valuable things should be paid for.

On music royalties, *The Guardian*, November 5, 2014

In this business you have to develop a thick skin, but I'm always going to feel everything. It's my nature.

InStyle, June 2011

I've never thought about songwriting as a weapon. I've only thought about it as a way to help me get through love and loss and sadness and loneliness and growing up.

Vanity Fair, April 2013

When I get an idea in my head, I can't go to sleep. I have to finish it. And then I'll edit it for days, thinking about making it work perfectly.

Washington Post, February 8, 2008

It's kind of exhilarating, walking through a crazy, insane mob. The most miraculous process is watching a song go from a tiny idea in the middle of the night to something that 55,000 people are singing back to you.

Rolling Stone, August 1, 2013

One of the things people don't really recognize about the similarities between country and hip-hop is that they're celebrations of pride in a lifestyle.

99

The Guardian, October 18, 2012

For me, genres are a way for people to easily categorize music. But it doesn't have to define you. It doesn't have to limit you.

The Boot, January 16, 2013

I have to practice to be good at guitar. I have to write 100 songs before you write the first good one.

Vanity Fair, April 2013

The youngest country artist to write a No. 1 song, Taylor Swift was only 14 years old when she wrote "Our Song" and she played it at her ninth-grade talent show.

The music video was also named Video of the Year at the 2008 CMT Music Awards.

You need music when you're missing someone or you're pining for someone or you're forgetting someone or you're trying to process what just happened.

Entertainment Weekly, October 15, 2015

66

My imagination is a twisted place.

99

Rolling Stone, February 4, 2010

66

Every one of my regrets has
produced a song I'm proud of.

99

Marie Claire, September 2013

In 2004, Taylor performed at the Bluebird Cafe in Nashville and met Scott Borchetta, which eventually secured her a contract with Borchetta's Big Machine Records in 2006.

In October that year she released her first album, which sold more than 2.5 million copies.

CHAPTER
TWO

FRIENDSHIP

From the enchanted world
of fairytale love to squad goals,
here are Taylor's words
for her friends and family.

I love making new friends
and I respect people for a lot of
different reasons.

Marie Claire, June 22, 2009

Fans are my favorite thing in the world. I've never been the type of artist who has that line drawn between their friends and their fans. The line's always been really blurred for me. I'll hang out with them after the show. I'll hang out with them before the show. If I see them in the mall, I'll stand there and talk to them for 10 minutes.

Taylor Swift: The Rise of the Nashville Teen
by Choe Govan (2012)

Noted for her close-knit girl squad, comprising celebs like Selena Gomez and Blake Lively as well as models from Taylor's debut on the Victoria's Secret runway in 2014, she is equally known for having feuds and making up—like with former frenemy Katy Perry.

You may leave behind friendships along the way, but you'll always keep the memories.

Elle, March 6, 2019

If you go too far down the rabbit hole of what people think about you, it can change everything about who you are.

Glamour, September 30, 2012

I think it's important to be self-aware about what people are saying about you, but, even more so, be very aware of who you actually are, and to have that be the main priority.

"All Things Considered," National Public Radio, October 31, 2014

I'm not that complicated … All you need to do to be my friend is like me … and listen.

Liner notes, *Taylor Swift* (2006)

I'm the girl who—I call it girl-next-door-itis—the hot guy is friends with and gets all his relationship advice from but never considers dating.

Teen Vogue, March 2009

I think that you can love
people without it being the
great love.

InStyle, November 2013

I'm not the girl who always has a boyfriend. I'm the girl who rarely has a boyfriend.

MTV.com, November 17, 2010

When you are missing someone, time seems to move slower, and when I'm falling in love with someone, time seems to be moving faster.

Billboard, October 19, 2012

I think every girl's dream is
to find a bad boy at the right
time, when he wants to not be
bad anymore.

Parade, November 25, 2012

I have rules for a lot of areas of my life. Love is not going to be one of them.

Rolling Stone, October 25, 2012

Part of me feels you can't say you were truly in love if it didn't last. If I end up getting married and having kids, that's when I'll know it's real—because it lasted.

Mirror, November 27, 2012

I don't think there's an option for me to fall in love slowly or at medium speed. I either do, or I don't.

Parade, November 25, 2012

But no matter what love throws at you, you have to believe in it. You have to believe in love stories and Prince Charmings and happily ever after.

Liner notes, *Fearless* (2008)

Relationships are like traffic lights. And I just have this theory that I can only exist in a relationship if it's a green light.

Wonderland, April 8, 2013

Deciding not to play games is the best way to go because it keeps things simple: If he messes it up by playing around with your heart, you'll know he doesn't deserve you. You were real with him, and he didn't return the courtesy. Someone else will!

Seventeen, 17 August 2013

I've been careful in love. I've been careless in love. And I've had adventures I wouldn't trade for anything.

Glamour, October 4, 2010

I think it's fearless to fall for your best friend, even though he's in love with someone else.

Liner notes, *Fearless* (2008)

"

Love is the one wild card.

"

Glamour, October 4, 2010

I think unrequited love is just as valid as any other kind. It's just as crushing and just as thrilling. I want you to remember that what you are doing is selfless and beautiful and kind. You're loving someone purely because you love them, not because you ever think you'll have your affections reciprocated.

To a fan, Instagram, July 2014

66

I never chase boys. They don't like it.

99

Elle, February 2013

I feel like watching my dating life has become a bit of a national pastime, and I'm just not comfortable providing that kind of entertainment anymore.

Rolling Stone, September 8, 2014

We should love, not fall in love, because everything that falls, gets broken.

Twitter, May 20, 2012

I think I am smart unless I am really, really in love, and then I am ridiculously stupid.

Vogue, February 2012

The drama and the trauma
of the relationship you have
when you're 16 can mirror the
one you have when you're 26.
Life repeats itself.

Women's Health, November 3, 2008

Here's what I've learned about deal-breakers. If you have enough natural chemistry with someone, you overlook every single thing that you said would break the deal.

Glamour, November 2013

I don't have a type. I don't have a specific kind of human being. It's just kind of an X-factor of sorts. Everybody I've ever dated has been a case-by-case situation.

Daily Beast, October 22, 2012

I've found that men I've dated who are in the same business can be really competitive. I've found a great group of girlfriends in the same business who aren't competitive, but a few times guys have started comparing careers and it has been ... challenging.

Irish Examiner, October 21, 2012

I love the ending of a movie where two people end up together. Preferably if there's rain and an airport or running or a confession of love.

Rolling Stone, October 25, 2012

… you grow up and you realize that Prince Charming is not as easy to find as you thought. You realize the bad guy is not wearing a black cape and he's not easy to spot; he's really funny, and he makes you laugh, and he has perfect hair.

On *Fearless* tour, April 2009

“

[Guys] can be a part of your life but never let the guy be your life. They can live in your world, but never make the guy your world. Knowing who you are and being independent and strong will be attractive to the right guy.

”

J-14, November 2012

I only write songs about crazy love. If I go on two dates with a guy and we don't click, I'm not writing a song about that. It didn't matter in the emotional grand scheme of things. There's a lot that goes on in daily life that isn't really worth turning into a verse and a chorus.

New York magazine, November 18, 2013

If someone doesn't seem to want to get to know me as a person but instead seems to have kind of bought into the whole idea of me and he approves of my Wikipedia page? And falls in love based on zero hours spent with me? That's maybe something to be aware of. That will fade fast. You can't be in love with a Google search.

Vogue, January 16, 2012

I feel jealousy, but I've been trying to channel it into mutual admiration and inspiration.

InStyle, November 2013

Just because you're happy in
a relationship doesn't mean
that there aren't moments
of confusion or frustration or
loneliness or sadness.

Telegraph, May 23, 2015

66

A good relationship is all about
balance and chemistry.

99

Hollywoodnews.com, October 31, 2010

Freeze-out. You don't respond to any of his texts or calls until he does something desperate [like] shows up. Or he calls and leaves a voice mail. Something that makes it very clear to you that he's interested.

On how to win the dating game, *Glamour*, March 2014

66

There are no rules when it comes to love.

99

InStyle, June 2011

CHAPTER
THREE

HEARTACHE

Whether it's game-playing and gaslighting, jealousy and lies or just your basic breakup, here's your therapy session courtesy of Tay Tay.

I feel like I get my heart broken more than break hearts.

Daily Beast, October 22, 2012

All of a sudden this person that you trusted more than anyone in the world is the person that can hurt you the worst. Then all of a sudden the things that you have been through together, hurt.

Vogue, December 9, 2020

I have had a guy say, as we were breaking up, 'You better not write a song about this.' At which point, I proceeded to write an entire album about it.

Daily Beast, July 14, 2017

Fixing your heartbreak by
getting into another relationship
is not the way to live your life—
you need to live it on your terms
for a while.

ASOS magazine, November 26, 2014

66

Red is such an interesting color to correlate with emotion, because it's on both ends of the spectrum. On one end you have happiness, falling in love, infatuation with someone, passion, all that. On the other end, you've got obsession, jealousy, danger, fear, anger and frustration.

99

New York Daily News, November 10, 2012

At some point, you grow out of being attracted to that flame that burns you over and over and over again.

USA Today, October 17, 2012

Don't worry. You may think you'll never get over it. But you also thought it would last forever.

Twitter, 15 August 2013

There is nothing wrong with avoiding people who hurt you. You fell in love, no games. Now you're saying goodbye with no games. Protect yourself, please.

To a fan on Tumblr, 2015

I've always said that the world is a different place for the heartbroken. It moves on a different axis, at a different speed. Time skips backwards and forwards fleetingly. The heartbroken might go through thousands of micro-emotions a day trying to figure out how to get through …

Tumblr, June 18, 2021

Good memories can leave even more of a scar on your heart than the bad times.

Twitter, September 5, 2014

Guys deserve what they get in my songs, and if they deserve an apology they should get one.

Parade, October 22, 2010

Guarding your heart and protecting your dignity are a little bit more important than clarifying the emotions of someone who's only texting you back three words. I've learned that from trying to figure out people who don't deserve to be figured out.

Glamour, February 4, 2014

If I meet someone who I feel I have a connection with, the first thought I have is: 'When this ends, I hope it ends well. I hope you remember me well.'

"All Things Considered," National Public Radio, October 31, 2014

You know what, it's like, when I find that person that is right for me, he'll be wonderful. When I look at that person, I'm not even going to remember the boy who broke up with me over the phone in 27 seconds when I was 18.

The Ellen DeGeneres Show, November 11, 2008

I don't want anyone to wait four hours to text you back and I don't want anyone to mess with your head. I want you to be happy … because waiting four hours to text someone back is rude. It's not flirting.

On *1989* tour, July 2015

Your feelings so are important to write down, to capture, and to remember because today you're heartbroken, but tomorrow you'll be in love again.

Seventeen, January 20, 2009

We think we know someone,
but the truth is that we only know
the version of them that they
have chosen to show us.

Prologue, *Reputation* (2017)

I've learned that just because
someone is cute and wants to
date you, that's not a reason to
sacrifice your independence.

New York Daily News, October 31, 2014

I can't deal with someone
wanting to take a relationship
backward or needing space
or cheating on you.
It's a conscious thing; it's a
common-sense thing.

Cosmopolitan, December 2012

I think everyone should approach relationships from the perspective of playing it straight and giving someone the benefit of the doubt. Until he establishes that this is a game. And if it's a game, you need to win. The best thing to do is just walk away from the table.

Glamour, March 2014

The singer famously writes about her romantic relationships in her songs, and her celebrity exes include Joe Jonas, Taylor Lautner, John Mayer, Jake Gyllenhaal, Conor Kennedy, Harry Styles, Calvin Harris, and Tom Hiddleston.

"

I think the worst part about a breakup sometimes, if one could choose a worst part, would possibly be if you get out of a relationship, and you don't recognize yourself because you changed a lot about yourself to make that person like you.

"

Hollywood Reporter, October 17, 2012

You will actually move on and
you actually will be fine and
then that's when he may actually
miss how incredible and special
you are.

To a heartbroken fan, Instagram, July 2014

66

The trick to holding on was all that letting go.

99

Vogue, January 2018

CHAPTER
FOUR

PROUD & LOUD

Taylor at her most fearless:
here she stands up for others,
tells you how to stand up for yourself,
and deals with the bullies
and haters.

No one gets to have a place in your mind if they weren't invited there by you. So please do me this one favour: Don't let their ugly words into your beautiful mind.

Tumblr, January 2015

66

People cut other people down for entertainment, amusement, out of jealousy, because of something broken inside them or for no reason at all. It's just what they do, and you're a target because you live your life loudly and boldly.

99

Instagram, September 2014

You should not be blamed for waiting 15 minutes or 15 days or 15 years to report sexual assault or harassment, or for the outcome of what happens to a person after he or she makes the choice to sexually harass or assault you.

TIME, December 6, 2017

My hope for the future, not just in the music industry, but in every young girl I meet … is that they all realize their worth and ask for it.

Wall Street Journal, July 7, 2014

I learned to stop hating every
ounce of fat on my body ....
I work on accepting my body
every day.

Elle, March 6, 2019

> **"** I now can really recognize and diagnose toxic messages being sent to me by society, by culture about my body. I'm a woman; I'm not a coat hanger. **"**

Interview with *Vogue* editor Edward Enninful, December 5, 2019

Grow a backbone, trust your gut, and know when to strike back. Be like a snake—only bite if someone steps on you.

Elle, March 6, 2019

People are going to talk about you. But maybe you're having more fun than them anyway. **99**

CNN, October 23, 2012

If they don't like you for being yourself, be yourself even more.

Huffington Post, September 3, 2014

In the last 10 years I have watched as women in this industry are criticized and measured up to each other and picked at for their bodies, their romantic lives, their fashion … It seems like the pressure that could have crushed us made us into diamonds instead. And what didn't kill us actually did make us stronger.

Woman of the Decade Award speech, December 12, 2019

Maybe you aren't meant to fit in. Maybe you're meant to stand out.

People, October 11, 2014

I want to still have a sharp pen and a thin skin and an open heart.

Miss Americana documentary (2020)

You are not the opinion of someone who doesn't know you. You are not damaged goods just because you made mistakes in your life. You are not going nowhere just because you haven't got there yet.

On *1989* tour, June 2015

Words can break someone into a million pieces, but they can also put them back together. I hope you use yours for good because the only words you'll regret more than the ones left unsaid are the ones you used to intentionally hurt someone.

Liner notes, *Speak Now* (2010)

Happiness and confidence
are the prettiest things you
can wear.

Twitter, February 13, 2012

Some days I totally appreciate everything that's happening to me, and some days I feel everyone's waiting for me to mess up.

New York Times magazine, November 16, 2012

As supportive as my hometown is, in my high school, there are people who would probably walk up to me and punch me in the face. There's a select few that will never like me.

Washington Post, February 28, 2008

When I am talking to people who I feel don't like me or are mean, I get really shy, and I kind of curl up personality wise.

Esquire, October 8, 2012

If a woman shares her experience in writing, she's overemotional. Or she might be crazy.

Barbara Walters interview, ABC, December 15, 2014

I saw that as a female in this industry, some people will always have slight reservations about you. Whether you deserve to be there, whether your male producer or co-writer is the reason for your success, or whether it was a savvy record label. It wasn't.

Woman of the Decade Award speech, December 12, 2019

Silence speaks so much louder than screaming tantrums. Never give anyone an excuse to say that you're crazy.

Glamour, February 4, 2014

Taylor is superstitious.
The number 13 is her lucky
number, as she was born on
the 13th, turned 13 on Friday
the 13th, and her first record
achieved Gold in 13 weeks.

The number 13 appears
on the decal on the nose of
her private jet and she writes
13 on her hand before
every show.

I don't like to feel like I'm some fragile package that has to be shipped by high-priority mail and handled with white gloves.

Parade, October 22, 2010

I think that it's okay to be mad at someone who hurt you. This isn't about, like, the pageantry of trying to seem like nothing affects you.

New York magazine, November 17, 2013

I never give advice unless someone asks me for it. One thing I've learned, and possibly the only advice I have to give, is to not be that person giving out unsolicited advice based on your own personal experience.

Billboard, May 25, 2013

Just keep doing 'you,' and being who you are and doing what feels natural to you.

MTV.com, October 1, 2014

It's okay to wonder how you could try so hard and still get stomped all over. Just don't let them change you.

To a bullied teen, Twitter, September 1, 2014

I'm thankful that when I go to bed at night, that I have been myself that day. And I have been myself all the days before that.

As seen on IMDb.com

Never believe anyone who tells you that you don't deserve what you want.

Marie Claire, October 16, 2015

I don't ever feel like the cool kid at the party, ever. It's like, 'Smile and be nice to everybody, because you were not invited to be here.'

Vogue, February 2012

People are going to judge you anyway, so you might as well do what you want.

Twitter, July 2, 2013

If you need to put me down a
lot in order to level the playing
field or something? If you are
threatened by some part of what
I do and want to cut me down
to size in order to make it even?
That won't work either.

Vogue, January 16, 2012

I want to wear pink and tell you how I feel about politics.
And I don't think that those things have to cancel each other out.

Miss Americana documentary (2020)

I don't really think about things as guys versus girls. I never have. I was raised by parents who brought me up to think if you work as hard as guys, you can go far in life.

When asked if she's a feminist, *Daily Beast*, July 14, 2017

Misogyny is ingrained in people from the time they are born. So to me, feminism is probably the most important movement that you could embrace, because it's just basically another word for equality.

Maxim, May 12, 2015

There is no such thing as a slut, as a bitch, as someone who's bossy, there's just a boss.

Miss Americana documentary (2020)

CHAPTER
FIVE

ON THE WAY TO GREATNESS

In need of motivation or inspiration? Taylor offers words of wisdom on success, failure, fame, and chasing goals and dreams.

A lot of people ask me, 'How did you have the courage to walk up to record labels when you were 12 or 13 and jump right into the music industry?' It's because I knew I could never feel the kind of rejection that I felt in middle school. Because in the music industry, if they're gonna say no to you, at least they're gonna be polite about it.

Entertainment Weekly, February 5, 2008

Every day was a struggle.
Forget making plans for life—
we were just trying to make it
to next week.

Rolling Stone, September 8, 2014

Be yourself, chase your dreams, and just never say never. That's the best advice I could ever give someone.

Taylor Swift: This Is Our Song by Tyler Conroy (2016)

I'm always afraid of failing.
I have to quiet that fear if I'm
going to get up in the morning.

Daily Beast, July 14, 2017

I'm intimidated by the fear of being average.

The Guardian, November 9, 2017

A multi-instrumentalist,
Taylor can play the guitar,
piano, ukulele, electric guitar,
and the banjo!

I would very much like to be excluded from this narrative.

Instagram, July 18, 2016

As soon as I accomplish one goal, I replace it with another one. I try not to get too far ahead of myself. I just say to myself, 'All right, well, I'd like to headline a tour,' and then when I get there, we'll see what my next goal is.

VH1, August 31, 2012

It's easier to get power than to keep it. It's easier to get acclaim than to keep it. It's easier to get attention than to keep it.

Rolling Stone, September 18, 2019

During her award for the 2009 MTV Video Music Awards' Best Female Video, Kanye West leaped to the stage, took the microphone, and declared that Beyoncé should have won.

When Beyoncé accepted her award for Best Video of the Year later in the show, she called Swift to the stage to finish her acceptance speech. West later apologized.

There's nothing quite like singing along to @ladygaga 'Paparazzi' while actually being chased by paparazzi.

Twitter, October 27, 2009

At a certain level of jetlagged, I just started answering all my business emails with 'I'll do whatever I want.'

Twitter, June 14, 2014

I want to make the most of this cultural relevance or success or whatever you want to call it, because it's not going to last.

Telegraph, May 23, 2015

To me, the safest thing I could do was take the biggest risk. I know how to write a song. I'm not confident about a lot of other aspects of my life, but I know how to write a song.

GQ, October 15, 2015

I don't compete with other people in the industry, I compete with myself.

Milford Daily News, May 28, 2009

Other women who are killing it
should motivate you, thrill you,
challenge you and inspire you.

Huffington Post, November 13, 2014

Anytime someone tells me that I can't do something, I want to do it more.

Teen Vogue, January 25, 2009

Giving up doesn't always mean you're weak. Sometimes you're just strong enough to let go.

Marie Claire, October 16, 2015

In my opinion, the only way to conquer stage fright is to get up on stage and play. Every time you play another show, it gets better and better.

CMT.com, November 12, 2007

I think the tiniest little thing can change the course of your day, which can change the course of your year, which can change who you are.

Seventeen, January 20, 2009

You can be accidentally successful for three or four years. Accidents happen. But careers take hard work.

GQ, October 15, 2015

You can make a board for all the goals you want in your life with the pictures on it, and that's great, daydreaming is wonderful, but you can never plan your future.

Wonderland, April 8, 2013

In 10 years of touring and writing albums, and having my confessional songwriting misunderstood, misconstrued, paraphrased, investigated, I've never wavered. This is the way I want to live my life.

NME, October 9, 2015

There are two ways you can get through the pain. You can let it destroy you, or you can use it as fuel to drive you: to dream bigger, work harder.

Marie Claire, October 16, 2015

Swift has, to date, won a whopping 32 American Music Awards and 11 Grammys, smashing several records for the most wins as artist and as female artist.

In total she's been nominated 924 times for awards or record holds, with 430 wins.

I've wanted one thing for me my whole life and I'm not going to be that girl who wants one thing her whole life then gets it and complains.

Taylor Swift: This Is Our Song by Tyler Conroy (2016)

When you're singing you can hear the echo of people in the audience singing every single word with you, and that was that big dream that I had for myself. It's happening.

DigitalSpy.com, November 22, 2012

You are the only one who gets to decide what you will be remembered for.

Foreword to *1989* (2014)

CHAPTER
SIX

KINDNESS & CONFIDENCE

Uplifting life lessons
on the value of being kind and caring
to others—and yourself.

"

It isn't history that makes heroes.
It's heroes that make history.

"

Marie Claire, October 16, 2015

66

Trying and failing and trying again and failing again is normal.

99

Elle, March 6, 2019

No matter what happens in life, be good to people. Being good to people is a wonderful legacy to leave behind.

On *Red* tour, September 2013

In 2011, Swift was named *Billboard*'s Woman of the Year.

In 2012, First Lady Michelle Obama presented Taylor with the Big Help Award for her dedication to helping others.

We don't need to share the same opinions as others, but we need to be respectful.

Seventeen, March 1, 2009

Fearless is not the absence of fear. It's not being completely unafraid … To me, fearless is living in spite of those things that scare you to death. Fearless is getting back up and fighting for what you want over and over again … even though every time you've tried before you've lost.

Liner notes, *Fearless* (2008)

When you hear people making hateful comments, stand up to them. Point out what a waste it is to hate, and you could open their eyes.

Huffington Post, August 11, 2017

My parents taught me never to judge others based on whom they love, what color their skin is, or their religion.

Seventeen, March 1, 2009

"

When you say 'control freak' and 'OCD' and 'organized,' that suggests someone who's cold in nature, and I'm just not … But I just like my house to be neat, and I don't like to make big messes that would hurt people.

"

Taylor Swift: This Is Our Song by Tyler Conroy (2016)

In life, you learn lessons. And sometimes you learn them the hard way. Sometimes you learn them too late.

NBC TV Thanksgiving Special, November 25, 2010

Just because there's a hurricane going on around you doesn't mean you have to open the window and look at it.

Seventeen, July 30, 2014

> **"**
> Apologizing when you have hurt someone who really matters to you takes nothing away from you. Even if it was unintentional, it's so easy to just apologize and move on. **"**

Elle, March 6, 2019

I have this really high priority on happiness and finding something to be happy about.

InStyle, June 2011

I've always been a hugger. If
we all hugged more, the world
would be a better place.

People, December 6, 2007

All I ever do is learn from my mistakes so I don't make the same ones again. Then I make new ones.

MTV.com, October 27, 2014

I realized there's this idea of happily ever after which in real life doesn't happen. There's no riding off into the sunset, because the camera always keeps rolling in real life.

Elle, June 2015

Banish the drama. You only have so much room in your life and so much energy to give to those in it. Be discerning. If someone in your life is hurting you, draining you, or causing you pain in a way that feels unresolvable, blocking their number isn't cruel. It's just a simple setting on your phone that will eliminate drama if you so choose to use it.

Elle, March 6, 2019

We have to live bravely in order to truly feel alive, and that means not being ruled by our greatest fears.

Elle, March 6, 2019

"

There is a time for silence, and there's a time for waiting your turn. But if you know how you feel, and you so clearly know what you need to say, you'll know it. I don't think you should wait. I think you should speak now.

"

Liner notes, *Speak Now* (2010)